FLYING ON THE INSIDE AND REACHING NEW HEIGHTS

The True Story Of The Wise Entrepreneur

Frankie Kington

Cover design by Lisa-Marie Igbinovia

For my beautiful family with love –

my daughter, Candice Rose,
my mum, Venice Rose,
my dad, Franklin,
my brother, Michael,
my sisters, Jackie Kington and Jessica Houghton,
my cousins, Sharon and Eddie Lewis,
and my late grandparents, Carol and Ethlyn Lewis.

FOREWORD

I have gone through Frankie's lucid, wide-ranging challenges, assumptions and highlights and their consequences during his growing-up stage of life. It is a very personal story and speaks to where we are now. To help a new generation, who are aggressive and disruptive, Frankie rises from a place of knowing and respecting the experiences that have shaped him. Today as a public speaker with a mission in mind on behalf of Xross-Polynation, I wish him luck. Frankie is fiercely honest and from his lifetime of experiences of class and identity, he proves race and colour are no excuses for a new generation who are looking for a role model.

In addition to being a thought leader, Frankie is a thought-provoking author who respects intelligence and insight and is highly persuasive with a can-do mission statement. His personal history is about hope for the future and unspoken access to a contingent of Britishness through sports, culture, and arts entertainment. Frankie's glowing confidence in his talks agrees with his thoughts. How can black people remain second class citizens when our national football team supports so many black people? Frankie's experiences have shaped him in a real way to write his first book, which will inspire and educate the new generation who will be closely watching. As a public speaker and a proud British African, Frankie is asking them to shake off their inferiority complex by leaning on the majestic cultural history of Africa and its contribution to Britain, retaining its riches within the Commonwealth's new ideology.

During her long reign, the Queen, together with other members of the royal family, has witnessed different lives like colours of the rainbow. Also, Asians must now be encouraged to dig deeper into their unfortunate chapters on the history of the empire. Let's leave it to the historians to analyse and record. Let's not ask for any sympathetic victims' attitudes based on historic facts. Instead, let us embrace an attitude of uBuntu, the spirit of humanity and community, and combine it with our actions which will speak louder than words.

The distinguished cultures and their diversity are what Frankie believes in and the Xross-Polynation community is proud to endorse him as its public speaker. The key strength of our creative practitioners, who are at the forefront, stands firmly in their own light as individual manifestations of the thinking process of the dynamic experiences undertaken. To this effect, the audience is advised to start and invest their peaceful actions, not only as they stand before us but also in the potential of what they point to in the future.

Ravinder Kalsi MFA (International practice) FRSA, SAR

Founder member and Managing Director
of Xross-Polynation Art Gallery.

With Grace and Gratitude.

"Peace is a journey of a thousand miles, and it must be taken one step at a time."

Lyndon B. Johnson

CHAPTER 1

My Early Childhood in Manchester

"We need leaders not in love with money but in love with justice. Not in love with publicity but in love with humanity." Martin Luther King, Jr.

Hello, my name is Franklin Esidore Kington, and I was born in the great city of Manchester, in an area called Gorton. April 29th 1969 was a great day for the United Kingdom - a hero was born into the world! I was born at 16 Cecil Grove, the house in Gorton where my grandma, Ethlyn, and my grandad, Carol, lived. My grandparents had two children - my mother, Venese, and my mum's brother, Edgar, who was my uncle.

Looking back, we were a close-knit family, brought up with a lot of faith and Christian values. Before eating dinner, we always used to say the Lord's Prayer. Every Sunday, we would go to church, where we all had responsibilities. My grandad was a churchwarden for over 25 years, and I carried the cross into the church for 23 years. My brother, sister and I all sang in the church choir.

In 1969, I lived in a place called Ardwick Green in Manchester. I lived there with my mum, my brother, and my sister in a three-storey block of flats called Fort Coverdale. Our three-bedroomed flat was lovely to live in. I have a lot of happy childhood memories from Ardwick Green. I would play outdoor games with my brother in the park at the back of our flats. At home, we'd sit on the floor, play board games, and have lots of fun. I was always a very competitive kid who liked to win!

My primary school was called Ross Place. I was excited to find out that Harry H. Corbett had attended my primary school when he was a boy. He was a famous comedy actor who starred in the comedy series *Steptoe and Son,* which was shown on television in the 1970s. This is where I had dreams to be famous like Harry H. Corbett because he was so funny and a great actor. He was my first role model. Knowing that he had become famous after living in the same area as me and going to the same school helped me believe that I could achieve great things in life.

I was always a shy kid who found it extremely difficult to concentrate at such a young age. This led me to mess around in primary school, getting into trouble with other children and teachers. I used to talk during lessons and would throw paper and pens at other kids when I was meant to be concentrating. I would torment the other children with words and the odd silly joke. This led to punishment from my teacher for my bad behaviour. I would be either strapped or slippered. The former involved being hit by a belt, the latter with a trainer. I became quite an emotional child, and developed 'bad boy' habits in school, bullying weaker kids who were struggling.

I was a troublesome kid, and my mother knew this. At this time, my home life was having an effect on my education. After ten years, my mum and dad's rocky relationship started to take its toll and my parents decided to end their marriage. This affected me deeply, but I still loved my mum and dad dearly. I felt confused, wondering if I could still have the same love for my mum and dad now that they had split up. I wondered if my dad would still love me. I blamed myself and started wondering whether something was wrong with me. My mum knew I was finding it difficult to get over the break-up because I was an emotional child, and my parents' separation was stirring up my emotions and causing more ups and downs than I had experienced before.

However, my parents' break-up made me stronger and moved my life in a different direction. Certain events in your life challenge you to grow strong, and this event certainly helped me to develop a strong character. It taught me to be happy and succeed in life, and not to hold grudges or blame anyone. Then I realised a big change in my life was going to happen.

When my mum told me we were moving away from Ardwick Green, because she thought it would be the best decision for our family's happiness, I felt sad. The area held so many fond memories for me and my family, the nostalgia was rich. In the years after I moved away, I still managed to see a lot of people who I had known when I lived there and who, like me, had now moved on to new areas. That made me happy. I was always blessed with strong family ties to protect me wherever I went.

CHAPTER 2

Who Needs Education?

"Success isn't always about greatness, it's about consistency. Consistent hard work gains success. Greatness will come." Dwayne Johnson

I n 1980, my family's life had taken a turn for the worse. My mum was struggling financially, so my gran and grandad decided to buy a house in Gorton where my family would live with my two cousins and my Uncle Edgar, who everyone called Eddie. Nine members of my family moved into an enormous house with six bedrooms, an attic and a cellar - I was coming back home - yippee!

I was so excited to live with other members of my extended family. I have even happier memories of my childhood years living there. We used to play football in the park, and they used to call us the Brazilians because we were that good! At home, we would play indoor games, chasing each other around our big house. It was even big enough to play a decent game of hide and seek!

The area I lived in was a predominantly white working-class area. That wasn't a problem, until we started to experience racism on a deep level. Not only was racism bad in Gorton, it was also bad at school. I remember being called derogatory names in the street and in the school playground. I spent the last year of primary school at a school called Old Hall Drive in Gorton. I had my struggles there, especially in Maths where my marks were very low, but I left relatively happy and content.

I was excited to be starting secondary school in September 1980. My secondary school, Spurley Hey High, was right next to Old Hall Drive school. My brother and two cousins already attended the same school, so I didn't feel alone in a great big new school.

I noticed from an early age that even though I was proud of who I was, I was treated differently from other people by the teachers and other pupils because of the colour of my skin. I felt I got on with a lot of people in my school because I had a warm personality but sometimes, I congregated with the wrong crowd - the kids who were getting into trouble for fighting with kids from other schools and turning up late for classes. I experienced a lot of racism. Other kids would torment me about the colour of my skin, which at times brought me to tears, but I realised I had to stick up for myself a lot of the time, which could prove to be difficult. The name calling made me angry and the bullying started to creep in, so sometimes I would end up in a fight and would be given detention.

I enjoyed outdoor pursuits and did this every year, going to the Lake District, a national park north of Manchester, dotted with serene lakes, rugged mountains and pretty villages in the beautiful countryside of Cumbria.

We stayed in youth hostels, doing activities like canoeing, mountain climbing, walking, and abseiling. I loved outdoor pursuits; it was exciting and exhilarating, and I always felt an adrenaline rush. It was like a school holiday, even though it was still part of my education at Spurley Hey High School!

I also loved athletics. I was the best in my school at 100 metres, 200 metres and high jump, and I was always set challenges to achieve. I used to compete with children from other schools in my area and was always competitive to be victorious. Daley Thompson, a famous athlete, was my hero. He won the gold medal for the decathlon at the Olympic Games in both 1980 and 1984 and broke the world record for the event four times. He was a gentleman and a true winner. I looked up to him, because he was very competitive and had a 'never give up' attitude with a humility that made him the successful person he was.

Education was always a struggle. I was so easily distracted in school, and I always ended up in trouble or had to stand outside the classroom door for misbehaving. Every year, exams were difficult, with low marks for my efforts. As I grew older, I was put on an Alternative Curriculum programme for kids who had learning difficulties. Around 100 kids were on the same programme, and because of this we used to get bullied and picked on a lot. Maybe these circumstances made me more determined to succeed in life and reach the top against all odds, despite the obstacles plus hurdles.

At such an early age, I began to develop bad habits inside school like smoking cigarettes and smoking pot. My friends would sometimes bring the odd joint into school, and we smoked it on the school field at break and lunch times. I was intrigued by smoking and the buzz it gave me –

that feeling of getting high. The odd joint started to become more like a joint a week, and I could see this pattern becoming worse for me in my social life outside school.

At home, I enjoyed listening to music with Uncle Eddie in his bedroom. He had a collection of classic albums like *The Wall* by Pink Floyd and *The Best of Hits* from The Doors.

In 1984, at the age of 15, I visited Glastonbury Rock Festival with school friends, and my Uncle Eddie went with us. That was an experience of a lifetime! We had planned this for ages, knowing Glastonbury was one of the biggest rock festivals in the UK. I was quite open about telling my parents where I was going, because the festival was about amazing musicians from all over the world coming together through love and peace. I had the opportunity see bands like New Order, Ben E. King, Misty in Roots, The Bundhu Boys and so many more. It was like a drugs festival, full of camaraderie and good cheer. I have never taken so many drugs in my life: acid tablets, dope, magic mushrooms - the list goes on, but it was one of the best times in my life.

The day before we went to Glastonbury, a friend of mine at the time experienced a near-to-death experience with a Class A drug called speed, a type of amphetamine. We walked him around the block of houses where he lived for two or three hours, knowing that if we were to let him sleep, he may not have woken up. He was so grateful we didn't let him sleep that night. This experience seriously frightened me. I thought, *I will never inject drugs in my arms. It's too dangerous; you don't know what you are injecting in your body.*

So, now you can see where my life was heading and the direction I was going in. Welcome to the wild days ahead! Going out at the weekends was always fun, but now, with my new habit of smoking cannabis, my life became a bit wilder. When you pick a new habit up, it's funny how you notice that a lot of other people are doing the same thing as you, because they seem to stand out. I started smoking dope quite regularly, getting high when I could, and it made me laugh a lot. You could smell cannabis on a person's clothes, especially mine!

This must have had an effect on my concentration levels, not just at school but in my social life as well. Drugs were so common when I was growing up, just like now in society. It was the 'in thing' to take drugs, people saw it as cool to chill out. But remember cannabis is a medicine and men like to abuse drugs to get high, experimenting all the time. My grandparents always used to drink cannabis in their tea and coffee. They did not consider it to be a drug. In their culture, cannabis was regarded as a medicine that would help prevent illnesses. They called it 'brain food'.

Let me tell you that alcohol and cannabis don't mix well, not for me. Certainly, lager combined with cannabis is not a good cocktail at all. The number of times I used to throw up on drink and drugs wasn't good for me. Being sick isn't a nice experience so I managed to stick to wine and whisky, which I loved. I could drink that till the cows came home. Was I an alcoholic? Well, I know a few girls I used to go out with said I was. Who needs education when you can drink and take drugs?

CHAPTER 3

The Needle in the Buddha

"Our greatest glory is not in never failing, but in rising up every time we fail." Ralph Waldo Emerson

It was now coming up to the year 1986. Do you know what year that was? The year I left school, going into the big wide world full of 'confidence and enthusiasm'. Or so I thought. What did Franklin Kington want to do when he left school? He wanted to be an electrician, and to be an electrician you had to be good at Maths. Well one subject I was not good at was Maths. Oh no! Shock, shock, horror, horror - what was I going to do? I was so naughty that I used to get thrown out of the lessons preparing us for our exams, but I knew the girls like a naughty boy.

My mum took me to Openshaw Technical College because I had an interview there to enrol on an Electrician Course. I was so excited! Yes, I was going to go to college to further my education - that was cool. There were around about 20 kids in the classroom, including myself, waiting to sit the entrance exam.

'Let's get started,' said the teacher. Looking at the exam sheet, I knew I wasn't going to pass this exam, but to my surprise not one of the kids in that room passed the exam either! It saved my embarrassment of failing - I knew there was one kid who was still doing the exam and so hadn't received his result back - but my disappointment was there to be seen on my face. I was almost in tears when I heard the results; it wasn't good enough. I went home that day absolutely deflated.

I knew a joint would ease the pain and take away the problem, well for a few hours, I thought, but the problem was still there. I went through a phase of asking myself, 'What do I do next?' I thought of all the things I was good at, like athletics. I should have pursued this further, but I didn't. Was my lack of confidence showing up in my life? I needed the extra push but felt I didn't get this. As my life started to get boring, sex and drugs and rock 'n roll kicked in daily for me. Soon, that buzz of getting high was wearing off. I felt I needed a 'bigger buzz', something different, something more scary or daring, a new adventure, a new drug.

I had seen it all now: cannabis, hot knives, a bong, a blowback, a chillum, solvent abuse. My friends and I knew so many different ways to get high. But was this buzz good enough for me or did I need more? What was that 'more'? I saw so many school friends putting needles or syringes into their arms to abuse either heroin or amphetamines.

What if I tried this? What would the consequences be? Well, you never know if you don't try, so I did. The first time my friends let me try speed, I enjoyed the feeling of it piercing through my veins and blood. We used to call it a 'rush', and it was certainly like that. Wow, that feeling! I felt my head hit the roof. Now I was feeling like Superman flying through the air! 'Look at me taking amphetamines in my arms, I am a cool kid!' Well, I thought I was. 'You can't touch Frankie Kington, he is Superman putting amphetamines in his arms. I bet you can't do that, you're not brave enough, you can't handle it!' But could I? I realised I wasn't sleeping and because of this I felt myself hallucinating sometimes. One thing that I was proud of, though, was that during all my wild years on drugs, I never robbed anyone to get drugs, because I always had money in my pocket from working. I always used to work. At that time, I worked in the Post Office industry as an office clerk. My mum insisted that I had to work, which I was comfortable with.

My family had seen a massive change in me and was wondering if I was up to no good. They would say things like, 'Frankie, I notice you are getting home quite late. Have you been to a club?' Or they would say, 'You look tired. Are you getting any sleep?' I ignored their concerns, saying I was actually fine and don't worry about me, but my behaviour was becoming very irrational and out of character. Even my Uncle Eddie was concerned, and he used to be addicted to heroin. *Leave me alone, I am fine*, I said to myself, still thinking I was Superman. Looking back, I would probably say those last six months on drugs were the darkest days. I was getting worse and worse and worse.

One Friday night, I went out with a friend from school. I had just had a fix of speed (amphetamine) and was feeling like Superman again. My friend and I had a night out in the most famous club in Manchester, The Hacienda. Wow, I was 'off my tree' on speed, just like my friend. We had a great night and I arrived home at around 4 am in the morning.

The next day I woke quite late, still 'coming down' from the night before. I was still tired and exhausted due to lack of sleep, but I did not feel the same. I felt extremely paranoid and scared as I lay in my bed in my room. I started to hear these horrible noises all about myself; my name was called a lot of the time. I felt like a paranoid schizophrenic, as the noises were getting worse and worse in my head and the extreme paranoia was horrible. I was so scared that I didn't want to get out of my bed, but I knew I had to. I cannot remember even going to the bathroom, but I knew I had to get out of my house.

It was a very cold Saturday morning, and I was tired. Where was I going to go? The only place I could think of was my dad's house in Rochdale. I needed to get away from Gorton for a few weeks. I was feeling like I never ever wanted to experience this feeling again in my life. I got on the bus on Hyde Road to go to my dad's. The bus ride was very scary and challenging. I remember sitting in my seat and feeling as if it was snowing inside the bus. Then, all the other passengers turned around and started staring at Frankie Kington. It was a horrible experience. I was coming down from the drugs very badly with horrific hallucinations. I kept hearing my name being whispered at the back of the bus. I thought to myself, *I have to get off this bus as quickly as I can.*

The next stop was the train station - Victoria Station in Manchester city centre. I was not looking forward to the train journey to Rochdale. I remember sitting on the train and this girl kept staring at me. I tried to ignore her but she kept moving her head so I couldn't avoid looking at her. Then she started laughing very loudly at me with her friends. This was a horrible experience! I started to shake a little bit through being cold and heard more strange noises of my name being mentioned on the train. I just needed to get to my dad's very quickly to come off the drugs once and for all.

That was it, never again! I decided at that moment: no more needles, no more speed. That experience of travelling to my dad's shook me up and frightened me in the sick condition I was in.

I arrived at Dad's around 3 pm. 'Hello, Dad,' I said. My dad looked at me as if to say, 'Hello son, you never told me you were coming over.' That was it - I broke down crying in front of my dad and his partner, Sheila. My dad knew there was something wrong, so he ushered me into his office in the garage to talk to me, and I told my dad what the problem was.

Straightaway my dad blamed everyone, even my uncle Eddie. He always felt I was hanging around with the wrong people and had encouraged me to go back to school and study. He was concerned about me, and he was upset I was not well. He could see I was cold and withdrawing from the drugs, so he left me alone for a few hours to let me come down from the drugs and get them out of my system, plus he had to work on a Saturday. I remember sitting in his office and hearing my name on the radio saying how paranoid I was. He had a plastic spider in his cup on the table and this started coming alive. It started wiggling its legs. I knew it was in my mind because of the drugs, but it was not nice to experience it.

I stayed at my dad's house for a whole month and was signed off work with depression. Dad and I cried a lot and shared a lot of nostalgia from the past. The next step was to pluck up the courage and admit I was a 'drug addict' and I had a 'problem'. My dad asked me questions like, 'Where did you get your drugs from? Were these friends from school?

How long have you been doing this?'

My dad told me to stay away from these guys. He said I could stay at his house whenever I wanted, and he would find me a psychiatrist to talk to. 'Get as much help and support as you can,' he advised me. This was the fastest way to resolve the problem. Now I knew the biggest step to take was to let the rest of my family know of my drug habit, then announce to my friends why I had been away for four weeks. This behaviour had to change quickly for my own good.

CHAPTER 4

Darkness Always Turns to Darkness

"Only in the darkness can you see the stars." Martin Luther King Jr.

F ast forward four weeks and it was time to leave my dad's. It was time to go home and face my family, my 'demons', and the outside world. Before I faced my family, I was quite nervous. They knew something was wrong, but they didn't know exactly what it was. So here we go, the moment of truth, I thought. I opened the door slowly and walked into the living room. They jumped up to hug and kiss me. The odd tear was shed, and my family were happy to see me. I knew my mum had phoned the police to make sure I was alright, because she was very worried, as were my brother and sister. I was absolutely fine and had let them know this when I was staying at my father's.

Everyone sat in the living room, with their eyes fixed on me, eager to hear what I had to say. You couldn't hear a pin drop, and then I took a deep breath and told them about my erratic six months of drug abuse. I could see and feel the expressions of sadness and regret about what had been happening to me at this time in my life. I put my arms around my head and cried like a baby, waiting for someone like my mum, brother or sister to hold me. I felt ashamed, but my family was so supportive. They helped me beat this horrible addiction.

Without them, I wouldn't be telling you this story, so a lot of gratitude and love goes to them for their support. At 18 years of age, I was too young to die. It brought me and my brother, Michael, closer. He looked out for me. We had a lot in common like playing football and family games. I also became closer to my sister, Jackie. At that time, she was a student at university and training to be an actress. She was feisty and highly educated. My cousins, Eddie and Sharon, were also very close to us all. Everyone was very supportive, warm, and understanding because that is how my family had brought us up - to love and respect everyone from the heart, no matter who we meet.

The next step was to tell my friends about my habit, especially the people closest to me at this time. Some of them knew how I felt, and some of them started to look out for me, so that I would stay away from the junkies. They did this by asking questions and monitoring my attitude and behaviour every day. There was no doubt that I had to stay away from certain people if I was going to kick this habit. As I did that, I started to get stronger and stronger. I tried to rebuild my life. I started going to the gym, walking, and reading books. I got myself well again with some help from outside organisations. I checked in with a psychiatrist, psychologists, and anyone else who could help me. I was certainly back on the road to some kind of normality. Opening up and talking to people in professional roles gave me the clarity I needed. Thankfully, I wasn't losing my mind.

They were dark days, and I would say they lasted 12 months. Sometimes, it felt like being in a bottomless pit or going through a dark tunnel waiting to see the light. However, this period of time helped me focus and get better at living my life. I have to admit that I did a lot of apologising to so many people for my behaviour. The apologies were accepted emphatically. I was living my life again, or was I? I was still smoking the odd joint, but as long as I wasn't putting needles in my arms, I knew I was going to be okay. I was still going to late-night parties and buzzing off my head, but not dangerously abusing my body. Now it was time to abuse my head with cannabis. The odd tablet here and there with the ladies really helped my buzz. My Uncle Eddie was very protective of me because we spent so many days off our faces on magic mushrooms just for a laugh, and it was very funny.

You have heard the saying time flies when you are having fun. My life was very enjoyable. I was the kind of person who was never in one place too long. I learnt to drive and started driving at the age of 21 in 1991. I was independent and could go where I wanted to, and that's how I enjoyed my life. I used to drive to a lot of clubs, enjoying myself with my friends, and my brother and uncle. Late-night rave parties were amazing to me. I met so many different people and formed some fantastic friendships. However, I knew I was growing older and couldn't maintain this type of lifestyle for much longer, so I decided to grow up a little bit. I did feel I was at a crossroads in my life, but I wasn't prepared for how much my life was about to change.

By 1996, the rest of my family had started to settle down with their partners. My sister decided to move down to London to pursue her acting career; my brother settled down with his partner; my mum had moved on with her partner and so had my Uncle Eddie.

A lot changed in that year. My grandad retired from the newspaper he used to print - *The Reporter* in Ashton Under Lyne. The large house in Gorton was costing us too much, so we decided to sell the house and move on in our own directions. I ended up moving to another area of Manchester - Clayton - with my mum. This was also a very challenging area to live in. There was a lot of unemployment there. Our house was robbed, and my car was broken into. Nothing ever lasts forever, especially the good times, but we were always close considering the problems our family had to face and overcome.

Most of my family had settled down, and they had new families to think of and live with. Uncle Eddie lived just down the road with his partner, and my uncle and I still enjoyed the closeness and togetherness of the family. Does darkness always turn to darkness? This cannot be right!

I remember going to bed after work one night, not knowing that the next day was going to change my life again. Early in the morning, my mum's boyfriend at that time popped his head around the door to tell me that Uncle Eddie had collapsed at home and had been rushed to hospital. I couldn't believe it! I jumped up out of my bed and raced to the hospital to see my uncle. When I got there, my grandad was reading the bible, so I knew this was serious. My Uncle Eddie had collapsed in the shower after suffering a brain haemorrhage. He died in hospital. He was only 46. To lose someone I loved so much at such a young age was traumatic for me. The whole world was devastated - that's how popular my uncle was.

I was so angry and frustrated - it felt like I was having a nervous breakdown! The pain of losing someone who I was very close to was heart-breaking and upsetting. I thought I was going mad. I wanted the whole world to stop and feel my pain. My lovely grandad, whose son had just died, was a tower of strength for the whole family. He was the 'man of the house' with distinguished gentlemanly characteristics. My grandad was very noble and upright, and he carried out his faith elegantly. The whole family were in so much pain. It was as if we were all losing our minds over this death. I know now that I didn't grieve properly, and have a guess what was going on in my mind? Darkness always turns to darkness.

CHAPTER 5

Darkness Eventually
Turning to Light

"I walk in darkness so that others may see the light."
Frankie Kington

The pain of my Uncle Eddie's death devastated everyone. I was in so much pain that I thought I was going mad. My whole family experienced the same feelings. My mother's only brother was on his way to heaven, the next life. Now we had to face life without Eddie Lewis. Wow, this took some adjusting to and some patience to achieve. Everyone was in so much pain about this ... what was I going to do? I was back in a state of depression.

We were very close, me and my Uncle Eddie. He was my best friend at that time. Let me tell you, we smoked a lot of dope, more than ever, and still hung around with guys who were on the wrong side of the law. One night, a few weeks after Uncle Eddie's death, I was at a friend's house when two of these guys came round – I knew them through friends. That was cool, they weren't threatening but were doing bad things. Maybe not as bad as some of the things I had done in the past, but they had bad habits. Does 'crack cocaine' come to your mind?

Yes, they liked crack cocaine and wanted to have sessions at my mate's house to say thank you for the space. What did I do? I had tried cocaine before, but not crack cocaine, so like a jerk, back to the darkness I went. I tried crack cocaine for the first time. It was easy to escape the pain of my uncle's death with my mate. I am sure you are following the story, guys. The same patterns were emerging. I needed to get away from my uncle's death, it was too painful, so crack cocaine would solve the problem. Or would it?

Me and my mate had our first pipe - this was absolutely amazing but straightaway I realised the dangers of taking this drug. I told myself I would be alright as long as I wasn't putting needles in my arms. Is that right, Frankie? A new drug but on a different level. This time, instead of injecting, I was now smoking crack cocaine in a pipe. This drug is supposed to be the most dangerous psychological drug on the planet.

What's going on, Frankie? Déjà vu, don't you learn anything? Now I was doing the weirdest things every time I had crack cocaine. The craving for this drug was ridiculous. I used to walk with my friends to the Moss Side area of Manchester to get this drug day in and day out. When our friends came around, what did they do? Crack cocaine! One night, a fight nearly broke out because a friend knocked a guy's cocaine line all over the floor. This was daft, Frankie. My internal dialogue went like this: *Calm down, calm down … I don't think so, the buzz is too good … I can handle it, oh yes!* I could not.

People always say they can handle something until it's too late. Spending nights arguing and falling out over-drugs isn't a nice thing to do but this was my life now. Everything was intense when it came to drugs. Drugs at work as a post office clerk, where I felt relaxed in a stress-ful job. Drugs at dinner, drugs in the evening, out in the pubs and clubs. Drugs, drugs, drugs, drugs glorious drugs. Psychologically, I was a mess in the morning, afternoon, and evening. There was no escaping it.

This lasted for about a year and messed my head up completely. I became very tired of taking crack cocaine. At midnight on New Year's Eve in 1996, I was on my way to Moss Side with a friend to score a hit of crack cocaine – we were planning to celebrate the New Year with a bang. That night, something said to me, 'Frankie, stop taking this drug! Uncle Eddie would certainly not be proud of you doing this. He's watching over you.' So, my friend and I de-cided to turn back towards home and stop this habit. How we did that, I don't know, but we did. I certainly stayed away from bad influences, but this kept happening to me - the same cycles and patterns - but the clue is that I am still here, fighting to tell you this story.

At this point in my life, I felt that I needed a complete change of scenery, so I knew I had to do some soul-search-ing to completely transform my life for the better. What were the first steps? Education. Who needs education?

CHAPTER 6

A Cat with Nine Lives

"Don't be afraid of being outnumbered. A lion walks alone while the sheep flock together. Be strong. Be you." Frankie Kington

H ave you ever felt like a cat with nine lives? I know what you're thinking - what does Frankie mean by this? Well, then, I'm asking if there have been events in your life when you have thought to yourself, My, oh my, that was a close shave! Maybe these incidents were a matter of life and death.

My first one was in 1979. I was playing out in Ardwick Green at the back of our block of flats. Did you know I stood on the copper bar inside a concrete slab? To my surprise, I slipped off this bar and it banged me straight in the face. My face was throbbing, and it swelled up because of the force of the bar hitting my face. I was fortunate; it could have done a lot more damage.

The second incident happened in 1981. At secondary school, I was playing a game in the playground. As I jumped over a wall to grab my friend, I slipped and banged my leg and shinbone. My friends carried me into the headteacher's room, where I waited with blood gushing out of my shinbone. The scene was horrific. I was lucky I didn't do more damage to my leg. I was taken to hospital and ended up having several stitches.

The third incident took place in 1982. I used to go swimming in a park near my house in Gorton called Debdale Park. My friends and I decided to go for a swim to the yacht in the middle of the reservoir. Halfway there, I lost my breath and started panicking. My friends tried to calm me down, but I continued to struggle for breath and thrashed around in the water. Fortunately, the driver of a speedboat had seen me panicking. He pulled me out of the water and took me back to the shore.

The fourth incident was in 1984. I used to hang out in Stockport with my friends, where we got friendly with a couple of guys we used to drink with. We ended up meeting some girls in Stockport. To our surprise, we weren't liked by a group of lads down there, so one night they decided to jump me and my friends in Stockport town centre.

One of my friends was punched in the face by a guy who had knuckle dusters on his hand. This marked my friend's face badly and left blood gushing from his head. By this time, the fight had spilled out onto the road, and luckily for me, I managed to dodge a bus that was moving in my direction by pulling my head back and throwing my body down onto the pavement. *That was a close encounter*, I said to myself as my back slammed onto the concrete.

The fifth incident followed in 1985. I got into a fight

with a guy. I punched him, and he went straight through a shop window. I was lucky to get away, because this wasn't meant to happen - it was an accident. I was being racially abused and I reacted.

The sixth incident also happened in 1985. A friend of mine was sniffing glue one night on Gorton market, near where I lived, so I had a go for a few hours and decided I didn't want to do that again. It wasn't a nice experience at all. Gas, I found, was more controllable. It gave me a funny buzzing sensation, but this addiction didn't last very long either. I knew it wasn't good for me at all. It made me dizzy, dazed, and confused. Both these incidents could have resulted in more dangerous consequences.

The seventh incident was three years later – in 1988, when I became addicted to speed (amphetamines). I was injecting drugs into my arms – this is a very dangerous way to abuse drugs. If you use dirty needles, it can cause septicaemia, known as blood poisoning. You never know what is in the powder; it could be rat poisoning, washing up liquid or flour, but remember some drug dealers may just want your money so you have to trust it is the drug you ordered. If not, it could cause an overdose or even death. I was very fortunate that this did not happen to me.

The eighth incident took place in 1992 near where I lived in Clayton. I was sitting in my mate's car when a man smashed the car window with a stick. The glass shattered in my face but, luckily for me, no serious harm was done; no shards were stuck in my skin, and I did not have any gashes on my face or neck. I was a little shaken up, but this incident could have been a lot more dangerous.

The ninth incident happened in 1996. I took crack cocaine which is a dangerously and psychologically addictive drug.

I remember all these incidents very clearly because any of these events certainly could have killed me or caused bigger effects in my life. I am sure I could also have touched on some other events in my life in which I had a narrow escape. Even during the school years of being bullied and getting into fights, I always came out unscathed and victorious. Through all these incidents, I always felt like there was something telling me about my life.

I felt that I had a reason to be here, rather than just getting high on drink and drugs, and blaming the world for my problems. I needed to get away from feeling like the victim and start taking full responsibility for my life.

Growing up in Manchester, I had to be streetwise because it wasn't an easy place to live, so looking after number one was a must.

My first decision to completely transform my life followed the ninth incident. I decided to go back to education in 1997 at the age of 27. My dad advised me to go into the world of Information Technology to learn computer programming. So, I started my first Course in Computer Programming at a college called Manchester College of Arts and Technology – or MANCAT for short.

I was so excited to be going back to school to learn computing, but there was a problem. I found it quite difficult to learn at first. Even more difficult was knowing there were students who didn't care, and they were messing about all the time. Kids were talking loudly and sitting on the desktops where the computer keyboards were stationed. They were playing games on the computers when they should have been working. My teacher wasn't the best, and I ended up making complaints. Despite my complaints, I left with nothing – no certification at all. Undoubtedly, this college wasn't as good as it could have been, but I used it as a stepping stone to do bigger things in IT.

For the next step, I started a course at an IT training company called Computeach, learning computer programming in COBOL, which is an abbreviation of Common Business Oriented Language. This was a more difficult course, and it was online. However, I managed to pass two courses in computer programming. They were Diploma and City & Guilds Standard Certifications.

At some stage, I was wondering whether computer programming was what I really wanted to do, because I couldn't find work, no matter how hard I tried. So, I went on to pursue a Computer Networking course in Salford, where I learnt a lot more about computers. I worked in Salford for 12 months and then worked at Fujitsu for three months. Did I like it? No, I didn't. I am not criticising the companies. I just felt it wasn't for me and decided to move away from working with computers.

So, I decided I would like to work for a company called Standguide. This was a great company where I learnt so much about myself. In my role as a placement officer, I worked with various organisations to place students in temporary positions at different companies. The students' roles were either work experience or internships. This job led me to better career intentions and more interesting jobs.

I even had six months' experience working as a Civil Servant for the Jobcentre. That was an experience of a lifetime. The stress levels were so high that if the health and safety officers had visited, they would have closed the place down. Not a good working environment. Arranging direct payments into customers' bank accounts over the phone proved to be very challenging.

Funnily enough, after that job, I ended up being a Security Officer for the largest security firm in the World, G4S. Not only that, I was offered the responsibility of management as well, which I gladly accepted. This led me to acquire some very useful skills, including customer service skills, customer care skills, conflict management skills, and first aid skills, giving me the skills to deal with all types of people. I had the responsibility of changing light bulbs, fixing plug sockets, mending damaged furniture, putting up signage in corridor areas of the building, and reporting odd jobs which needed doing.

CHAPTER 7

Manhood

"The quality, not the longevity, of one's life is what is important." Martin Luther King Jr.

This was the year 2000. It was the millennium year, the year that was going to change everybody's life for the better. Around this time, I began a relationship with a lovely lady called Marie. She lived five minutes away from me. After I had bumped into Marie a few times around Clayton, my next-door neighbour, who knew Marie, told me, 'She fancies you.'

I was always fond of Marie and fancied her quite a bit. We ended up having a relationship for around four years; I would to and fro from her house. As you can see, I started to settle down with her, and a lot of people got jealous of this. People began to stir up trouble, accusing us of something we hadn't done, backstabbing us, and criticising our relationship. I was growing up and having to change my life quite a lot. You already know about the educational side of my transformation, now it was the 'transformation of my manhood', because this was the year that was going to change everything.

While in a relationship with Marie, I used to work nights quite a lot so I would get home early in the morning, at around 6.30 am. I would then sleep at Marie's house until around 12 noon. I wanted to prove to Marie that I was a hard worker and worked for everything I had. Working nights and studying through the day taught me a lot about my own capabilities. It allowed me to see what I could achieve if I put my mind to what I really wanted out of life.

Marie came into our room one morning in July 1999 and said, 'Frankie, are you okay?'

I said, 'Yes, why? Is everything okay?'

'Yes,' she replied, 'but I have some good news to tell you. I'm pregnant.'

'Okay,' was all I could say before going back to sleep - uncharacteristically of me. I have never slept so long in all my life. I woke up at 4 pm, wondering what I was going to do with my new life. Wow, I was shocked, but when the news eventually sank in, it hit me - Frankie Kington - a dad, and then a broad smile lit up my face. I was going to be a dad - yippee!

I told all my friends and family the news - I was going to be a dad! They were all happy for me, excited and thrilled! Then I realised, *I am not number one anymore.* The next nine months definitely challenged my manhood and made me grow up quickly.

Even though I knew my life would change, it was going to change for the better. I prepared like any father would, knowing he is bringing a daughter or a son into the world. Life felt exhilarating and exciting because I knew my life was going to change again. One thing I did know was that Marie's health wasn't one hundred percent, so I did my best to protect Marie's life the best I could, knowing she was carrying my baby.

During her early pregnancy, Marie had to go to the hospital several times to be checked out because her doctor was concerned. I spoke to my cousin Sharon about this, and she warned me, 'Marie isn't well, Frankie. This isn't morning sickness.' At first, I paid no attention to what was going on. *It's just morning sickness*, I thought to myself. Then, Marie's condition got worse and worse and worse. About six months into the pregnancy, Marie took ill. She was bleeding from the inside. Now I knew this was serious.

Marie was called in urgently to North Manchester Hospital in Crumpsall. She was put onto a drip straightaway and was quite gaunt-looking and frail. I gave her all the support she needed for her life. I stayed at the hospital when I needed to. I had a conversation with Marie's doctor. He told me, 'We are going to have to operate on Marie or she is going to die with the baby.' Shock, shock, horror, horror, what was I going to do? Marie already had two children to two fathers, and I was responsible for looking after them. Plus, I had to go to work, so this situation was very challenging at that time in my life.

After I heard that Marie had to have an operation, I was feeling quite depressed and lost, quite sad and down. What I did know was that I had a lot of faith with my Christian values. Also, at that time, my sister was a Buddhist practitioner, so I knew her prayers would have a positive effect on my situation. I was quite anxious and feeling alone, but I had to keep the faith, though I knew this was quite challenging for me.

One day, I felt a sharp pain in my stomach just below my heart. I was struggling to breathe. Was I having a heart attack? Chantelle, Marie's daughter, called an ambulance, which took me to Ashton Hospital. I sat there virtually all night in a hospital bed.

Eventually the doctor saw me. I talked to him about what was going on in my life. I told him about Marie being in North Manchester Hospital with my baby and how ill they both were. The doctor said I was suffering from anxiety, and I had experienced a panic attack. He gave me some medical advice. Take some time off work and try to relax, breathing in and out slowly several times a day. What were we like? Me in Ashton Hospital, Marie in North Manchester Hospital with our baby, who were both not well at all. All I did know was that while Marie was fighting for her life and her baby's life, there was still hope that Marie and our baby had a chance of being alive and well in this world.

I started to see light at the end of the tunnel! Do you know they operated on Marie while her baby was still alive, and the operation was a success? Marie had to have medical intervention for at least two years after that, but believe it or not, my beautiful baby was still alive and kicking.

The doctors were amazed. They couldn't believe they had both pulled through the operation. It was like a miracle - this showed the power of faith and the human spirit. Marie's doctor was Spanish, and he even shared this story in a Spanish newspaper. Now that the whole family could breathe a sigh of relief after what had happened, I was even more excited. I was so proud of Marie and our baby. It felt like a massive victory that we had all won!

I honestly believe this event was challenging my manhood to see if I really wanted to become a father. Wow! Certain events play a major role in defining whether you are a real man, ready to take on responsibility. After the operation, Marie was getting bigger and bigger, and I went down to the hospital to see the scan of my little warrior. My, she was a fighter! I knew I wouldn't have to worry about her too much once she was in the world; she had her mother's fighting spirit.

So, nine months flew by and now we were ready for the birth of our daughter. The doctors said they would call me when the birth was imminent, or she was ready to start labour. The taxi driver, who I knew, said he would get me there in time for the birth. He did as he said! He put his foot down and drove me there in no time, ready for the birth. North Manchester Hospital, here we come!

There was Marie ready to give birth, or was she? Legs spread trying to push, but nothing happened at all. Marie started crying, saying she was in too much pain due to her medical intervention through the operation. So, the doctors said Marie had to have a caesarean birth. At this point, I was exhausted and started to cry. *What next, what next?* I thought. Then, the caesarean took place. Marie was holding my hand very tightly, and here she was, out popped Candice Rose Kington! I couldn't believe it, she didn't even cry - she was just staring at me with lovely big black eyes. I was thinking, *All that you have put me through for nine months and you're not even going to give me a tear.* Then, I thought, *Wow, you are beautiful and a tough cookie.*

I cried tears of joy - I was ecstatic! That was the day I changed into a proper man and now I would experience manhood.

CHAPTER 8

*Finding hope and a new
direction in life*

*"When we change, the world changes. The key to all
change is in our inner transformation - a change of
our hearts and minds. This is human revolution. We
all have the power to change. When we realize this
truth, we can bring forth that power anywhere, any-
time, and in any situation." Daisaku Ikeda*

We are now approaching 2001. The year 2000
proved to be a very exciting and eventful year
for me. A lot of me changed for the better that
year. I felt I had already made a lot of changes to my life –
changes that were making me into the responsible person
I believed I was destined to be. Sometimes you have to dig
deep to reveal the treasures in your own life. I still had a
long way to go but making that first step forward was the
most important thing I did.

What was to be the next stage in my new life? What did I need to change now in my life? I honestly believe that you reap the results of the seeds you sow. I honestly do believe that if you have faith in your life, the Universe will protect you and move your life in a positive direction, guiding you on your journey to happiness and success.

With my new life as a father, I felt I still had a lot to look at in my life. I had very strong Christian values but, deep down, I was realising they weren't helping my life at all. I felt I needed something deeper and more meaningful. I have always been the kind of person who thinks deeply and looks at life very deeply. I was looking for a different direction in my life, a new path to follow.

I discussed this with my sister who could strongly relate to the situation I found myself in. I came from a Christian family, yet I felt that Christianity was not working for me on a deep level. My sister advised me to carry on with practising Christianity for the time being whilst exploring other ways of finding meaning in my life. I was intrigued by the Buddhist philosophy of life she was following. It seemed so different from the Christianity we had been brought up with. I became quite curious about the practice and wanted to find out more.

My sister encouraged me to find out more, so I started to read SGI-UK's magazines and books on Buddhism. The more I learnt, the more excited I felt. I felt like this was going to be a new start for my life, a new beginning for me. I knew that my life had to change because it had become stagnant, dull and boring, and my mental health was not good at all.

After some time, I went to my first SGI-UK discussion meeting, which introduces SGI-Buddhism to guests. I felt welcomed, embraced and comfortable, although I was among strangers. The people there looked like normal, down-to-earth people, the kind of people you saw in the street every day. They were openly sharing their experiences of how SGI-Buddhism had changed their lives. I felt as if I could talk with them about anything. I felt as if I trusted them straightaway. This was unusual for me at the time. On that evening, I became convinced that this was the path I wanted to follow. I was excited to learn more and walk further down this path.

My mind was filled with questions. I wanted to know everything about this new art of living at once but of course this wasn't possible. For example, I wondered how long I should chant every day, and I was told that it was my decision. I could begin with just one hour per day and try it out for two or three months to see how it went.

It took me a quite long time to get into the rhythm of chanting, but the people at the meetings were kind and encouraging. They helped me to practise repeating the mantra, which I found very challenging at first.

When I started to chant, study and go to meetings, I found that it brought up all the negative areas in my life which I knew I needed to change and transform. It made me more responsible because I was now taking full control of my life, probably for the first time.

In the first two years, it was often a struggle to follow the practice every day, but I realised that my life was changing, and this was what I needed to go through to help me change for the better. So, I persevered with the practice and little by little I started to see positive results. Gradually, I realised that this practice was giving me what had been missing in my life up to that point.

The practice brought up a lot of changes in my life and made me challenge the company I was keeping. Not to say anybody was bad or wrong. I knew I had to move on, and sometimes you have to be around the right people who are going to respect you and help you to succeed in life without envy or jealously or trying to hold you back. This is all part of the process that helps you grow and develop a strong character.

The strange thing was that I no longer heard from any of my friends after I started practising SGI-Buddhism. It was as if I was being set free from my former life. I realised just how powerful chanting the mantra *Nam-myho-renge-kyo* was. The Universe was protecting me, moving me away from the drug scene and dangerous influences, into a positive direction. If this could happen so quickly, what else would happen if I practised every day for years?

I wasn't disappointed when I didn't hear from my friends. I realised this was a turning point in my life. More benefits of the practice revealed themselves in the ongoing transformation that was happening in my life. I discovered things in my life that I had never even dreamed of. The practice caused me to be more positive and focused, although I still had days of depression and sadness. I realised that I needed to go through those days in order to experience enlightenment. During those days, this quote from the Buddha gave me hope: "The lotus flower blooms most beautifully from the deepest and thickest mud." I realised that, like the lotus flower, experiencing all this darkness and depression would enable me to grow into a beautiful human being.

I had been practising for about a year and half when I realised that I needed to take full responsibility for my life and to get rid of the denial of this responsibility. I decided to commit myself fully to this philosophy of life by becoming a member of SGI-UK. I applied for membership of the organisation and my application was accepted. I received a Sanskrit scroll called a *Go-Honzon*, which is the object of devotion to my life. I began to pray to it each morning and evening to reveal my true and pure self. I also attended monthly discussion meetings where we chanted together, shared our experiences of the practice and supported each other through our struggles.

A friend of mine, who I grew up with and was close to as a teenager, was struggling with his life. He was intrigued because he had seen a recent change in me, so I invited him to an SGI-UK meeting in the Moss Side area of Manchester. He enjoyed the meeting and started to ask questions about how it could help him with his life. He practised SGI-Buddhism for about a year and went to meetings fairly regularly. Even though he stopped going to meetings for an unknown reason, he knew that SGI-Buddhism had made a huge difference in his life. I was happy that I'd encouraged him to become involved because it changed both our lives and moved us in a positive direction. I haven't seen him since, but I wish him well and hope that he is continuing to practise after the seed had been planted in his life.

At my very first meeting, I had thought that the room was filled with wise people. As I went to more meetings, I slowly discovered that all those people had struggles, problems, and challenges just like everyone else. I began to understand that SGI-Buddhism challenges you to look at all the negative areas of your life and deal with them. You have to be mentally, physically and intellectually strong to do that. I found out for myself that chanting helps you become not only strong, but also calm, serene, gentle, and disciplined. It also gives you a greater sense of self as you find out who you truly are, deep down. You discover that you have great potential within your life. After feeling hopeless, I began to feel hopeful.

From my own experience, I have found the main benefit of practising SGI-Buddhism to be self-transformation. I realised that my life was connected with the lives of everyone around me. I understood that we are all equal and we all have the Buddha nature within us. Buddha is another word for an enlightened person, or a hero of the world. It is so empowering to think that every single person in this world has the Buddha virtues of wisdom, courage and compassion lying in the depths of their beings to create a world at peace.

SGI-Buddhism has taught me that we, as human beings, have the capacity and the potential to create peace in the world. The current leader of Soka Gakkai is Daisaku Ikeda, who is known as Sensei, which means teacher in Japanese. I have chosen Sensei to be my mentor in life because he teaches me how to live sincerely and lead an upright and noble life. He calls on us as members of the organisation to carry the baton for world peace, the foundations for which he has already created.

I have found that gaining wisdom is another benefit of practising SGI-Buddhism, which gives you all the wisdom you need to move your life forward in a positive direction. That is where the title of this book, *The Wise Entrepreneur*, comes from. Wisdom changes everything. As long as you have wisdom, you can move everything in your life into a positive direction.

The practice has also given me courage. A Buddha, or enlightened person, needs to have courage as he takes on daring challenges in his life, as I have set out to do. If we are of the same mind as the Buddha, we have the potential in our own lives to create a world at peace by chanting *Nam-myho-renge-kyo*. This seems extraordinary, because it appears to be so simple, but I have found it to be true.

The practice has taught me to be more compassionate. Compassion is a state of life in which we care for everyone and everything on our planet, knowing that this is a true act of love and value creation. Compassion leads directly to enlightenment.

About a year into my practice, I started to see the good fortune and benefits pouring into my life. I was given more responsibility within the local organisation. This meant that I could attend a lot of meetings in the Greater Manchester area, supporting people though praying with them and giving guidance in faith to help them overcome problems that they faced in their lives. I have helped people overcome drinking problems, depression, and total despair in their lives.

I was happy to be part of Soka Gakkai, which is a Japanese word that means 'society for the creation of value'. The organisation is one of the biggest Buddhist organisations in the world, existing in 192 countries and territories. It is the most diverse gathering of people you will ever find on our planet. I do believe Soka Gakkai is playing an important role in bringing about peace on our planet. The organisation believes that world peace starts with each human being transforming him or herself internally and freeing themselves from negative forces.

I had changed a lot but there is always room for improvement, room to get better and better in your life. Life is about learning, growing, and moving in the right direction.

Nothing beats actual proof or real-life experience. As far as work was concerned, I knew I could do a lot more with my life than just working for the post office. I am not saying anything is wrong with this, but I always had this dream of being my own boss. I always had this dream of being very successful and becoming a millionaire.

How was I going to do this? I did not know, but I really needed to get out of my job. After working for 17 years in the same environment. I needed a new challenge in my life, and as you can see, I had already done some interesting jobs. Maybe I could work for myself and be my own boss.

Maybe I could be somebody who people looked up to, somebody who people could trust to help them solve a problem in their lives. As human beings, we all have problems and something that needs solving in our own lives. No one is perfect, but I respect the person who tries to do better the next day, and the next, and the day after.

I am the kind of person who likes to try new activities to see where it will take me and in what direction. I feel it's important to learn with a sense of curiosity, challenging yourself to do just that little extra each day, because you never know what you can reveal about yourself that has been hiding in your life for years.

The practice teaches you about why it is important to continue to study and learn. The capacity of our brain is infinite, so the potential we have is limitless and goes on into eternity.

After practising SGI-Buddhism for almost 19 years now, I can categorically say that this practice has changed my life for the better. The experience of chanting *Nam-Myoho-Renge-Kyo* has completely transformed my life on a deeper level. It has given me the confidence to reach out and fulfil my dreams as an entrepreneur and thought leader.

Life is about choices. What will you choose – to be happy or miserable? SGI-Buddhism has allowed me to make the choice to experience joy in every moment and every aspect of my life. The struggles have given me a greater appreciation for my life. I'm so grateful for my life as it is now because of the struggles I've been through and overcome. These have helped me grow as a person.

CHAPTER 9

A Professional Expert Authority

"A good coach can change a game. A great coach can change a life." John Wooden

I love studying, and I was very interested in the world of import and export, because it would open up the world to me and take me on many adventures. The world is a such a beautiful place with all its mysteries, filled with a rich variety of different cultures. I was eager to learn more about the world while improving my business skills, so I started an Import and Export course, which led me to an International Certification in Trading. Now armed with this experience and my knowledge, I started to attend meetings of a trading organisation called UK Trade and Investment – or UKTI for short - to help me understand how to negotiate deals around the world in different countries.

I met some very interesting people in UKTI and

attended some very interesting business meetings with people from East Asia. I learnt so much about East Asia and business negotiation, which would help me as an entrepreneur and thought leader in the future. I know from personal experience that networking and meeting people helps you develop the skills that you need to build confidence and grow as a businessperson, negotiating deals in your chosen field or profession. Everything you do at a meeting is being observed, so your behaviour is extremely important. Your attitude makes so much of a difference, allowing others to trust in you as a person to do business with. What if you could build a database of people to work with around the world, importing and exporting products into and out of different countries? This could be a very lucrative business and the skills you learn would be so valuable to you and your business.

At one International Trade Business meeting, I met a gentleman by the name of Christian. He was a nice person, and we connected instantly. We had a talk about a number of business opportunities, and he told me he knew a gentleman from China who he thought could help me in import and export. He wrote down his number, and I gave this gentleman a call. I managed to meet up with him, and we hit it off instantly! We talked for several hours and then decided to collaborate on ideas for importing and exporting goods from East Asia and Europe. We collaborated on some good business deals for products like mountain bikes, ladies' dresses, men's clothes, household goods and furniture. We had some clients and challenges, but I learnt a lot - enough to progress onto bigger challenges. It was another stage on my journey.

As an entrepreneur, you are always looking for ways to make money through good business venture opportunities that come your way. A very good friend of mine started working for a multi-level marketing (MLM) company called Utility Warehouse, and he showed me how it worked. Utility Warehouse deals with gas and electric, mobile phone and broadband services for your home, and they offer a number of other benefits as well.

I started to use their services for my home phone, broadband and mobile phones. They are an excellent company for home utility services and specialise in saving you money on all their services. They give you other benefits as well like a cashback card to save on your bills. After seeing the benefits of Utility Warehouse for myself, I decided that I wanted to share them with other people, so I worked for Utility Warehouse for several years. I attended all their networking events, and some of the people I met at this MLM Company were amazing. I found them so inspiring and warm, and I learnt so much from them.

I was starting to move forward in both my professional and private life, but I realised I needed to find the right mentor or coach who could help me direct my life into a positive direction.

Welcome Maria Kompanowski! Who is Maria Kompanowski? I met Maria at a Utility Warehouse networking event in 2011 - that's where our friendship started. When we bumped into each other at Utility Warehouse meetings, Maria and I always found time to say hello and get to know each other. We became good friends and mutual respect was there instantly. We used to go and have some food and a drink in the Asda café and, one Saturday afternoon, when I met up with Maria there, she told me that she was a business coach, as well as a distributor for Utility Warehouse. My first thought was, *Wow, I want to be a coach!* So, I asked Maria more about it.

She said that she had her own company called Dolphin Seminars, and she invited me to one of the meetings so I could see for myself what the meetings were about and whether the meetings were in line with where I wanted to be in my life. I went to the meeting, thoroughly enjoyed the seminar, and in no time, I chose Maria to be my business coach. I feel it was one of the wisest decisions I have made in my business career, because it has taken me to another level of expertise in business.

I also became a member of Dolphin Seminars, and this was another one of the wisest decisions I have ever made in my life. Not only was I being coached three times a week, I was also able to join a networking event every Saturday evening. I also started to attend Mastermind Groups with Maria, which give us knowledge and protect us when doing business so that we don't make too many mistakes. This is valuable information for anyone entering the world of business ventures or self-employment. I even got the chance to do presentations at business meetings which is very valuable for your confidence and growth. So, I was now beginning to make big strides in my development as a Professional Expert Authority.

At that time, I was a mentor, helping people with alcohol problems, mental health issues and other issues. I loved being a successful mentor and coach but really wanted to get involved in public speaking, which would propel my entrepreneurial skills to the next level. Around this time, in 2013, I became involved in an organisation called Toastmasters. Toastmasters is a public speaking organisation that trains you to be a professional speaker. With 332,000 members worldwide, this organisation is definitely bringing different people together from different nationalities and cultures all over the world. It is an organisation that is building trust around the world for people to keep speaking up about what they believe in. Toastmasters' core belief is that we are all gifted, unique, and courageously talented individuals, united through respect for one another.

This organisation provides training in communication, leadership skills, youth leadership, and public speaking through Accredited Speaker Programmes. It also organises speech contests, speakers' bureaux, conferences, and conventions.

I won a few speaking competitions with this organisation. One was entitled 'Weapons of Mass Distraction'. I learned a number of other skills, including competent communication and competent leadership skills. Being in this organisation helped me tremendously to develop my confidence in public speaking.

As you can see, all the skills I have now mastered have played a massive role in my journey towards becoming a Professional Expert Authority. Lifelong experiences in life shape you into the leader you believe you were destined to be.

I started to buy a lot of books at the Utility Warehouse networking events and learnt so much about successful entrepreneurs and thought leaders. Then I thought to myself, *Wow, I would love to be like them. With the right guidance and the right people around me, I could definitely do that!* I started to get inspired by great motivational and public speakers like Les Brown, Bob Proctor, Brian Tracy and Andy Harrington.

I looked at their lives and thought, *One day I am going to be just like them. I am going to inspire so many people to be successful and change their lives for the better.* How was I going to do this? How was I going to figure this out? One step at a time. First let me work on myself - let me be the shining light and example to everyone I meet! First of all, I had to figure out what was the first step. I realised when you are in business and start to want to work for yourself, the most important virtue is to take action and learn from people who are more successful than you and have made it in their professions and careers.

So, I started to do just that, and the first step, the experts told me, was to get into the habit of reading books. Books glorious books, there are so many of them and so many successful leaders and entrepreneurs. I noticed that they have all written a book. Many, many books inspired me, including Robert T. Kiyosaki's *Rich Dad Poor Dad*, Napoleon Hill's *Think and Grow Rich*, Dale Carnegie's classic *How to Win Friends and Influence People*, and *The Go-Giver* by Bob Burg and John David Mann. So that is why I am writing my book right now because I know I have an amazing story to tell that will inspire people to follow their dreams.

So why a book? A book builds trust with the people you want to work with. It shows you have a story to tell that will inspire people to open up. It reveals your inner qualities of how you have become successful and answers the question: 'Why should I want to work with you?' For me, writing a book is therapeutic when you reminisce about important events in your life that have changed your way of thinking and behaviour to make you the person you are now.

When you write a book, you open up to people with trust and honesty and reveal the darkest events in your life which can touch others. This is so important because we must encourage great and ordinary people to open up and release their pain inside for their own healing so that they can rebuild their lives.

I have learned so much about successful people's lives by reading their books, and it shows their lives are in no way different from ours. You realise that the greatest of people have experienced the greatest sadness or adversity on their journey to success. Now here's to your journey - see you on the other side!

CHAPTER 10

Appreciating Black African Art

"Art is an effort to create, beside the real world, a more humane world." André Maurois

In 2017, when I used to visit London regularly, I met a lady by the name of Ravinder Kalsi. Ravinder was a very smartly dressed lady, and every time I went to a business event in London, I kept bumping into her. When you keep bumping into someone at a meeting, have you ever had that feeling that there is a profound reason for it? Serendipity or synchronicity, call it what you will, but it kept happening to us. So, Ravinder and I decided to talk. We discussed a lot of subjects and found we had a lot in common. I found out that Ravinder was an expert in the field of Black African Arts. At that time, Ravinder had 25 years' experience in art history. She also has her own company called **Xross-Polynation**. This name represents all the different nations coming together through art. Xross-Polynation's mission is to encourage, appreciate and understand art and its role in society through engagement with original works of art.

When Ravinder mentioned that she had collaborated with the Royal Society of Arts and the United Nations, I thought, *Wow, this lady is well connected. She has a lot of experience and the support of so many well-known and famous organisations.* She was the person I had been waiting to meet, so I was stunned when she suggested straightaway, 'Why don't we set up our own organisation? You have a number of skills that you could adapt to this organisation.' She said, '**Frankie Kington, I need you.'** *Need me?* I thought. *Wow, Ravinder Kalsi, I need you!*

Ravinder and I managed to put something down in writing about what we planned for the coming years. This is what we wrote:

1. Art exhibitions - African culture and world arts – Ravinder Kalsi, CEO
2. Public speaking - Frankie Kington
3. Film and theatre productions
4. Multicultural dance and song shows
5. Online art/memorabilia sales
6. A talk show on famous African artists
7. A magazine, *Xross-Polynation*, with articles on creative contributions from the Commonwealth of Nations as well as philanthropists and benefactors. Our vision is to research and present the facts with no colour bar and in such a way to unite people of different faiths. Every issue will have an article from a Royal Society artist and/or a present benefactor of our society, Xross-Polynation.
8. Since it will be a community project, creative members,

such as well-established artists, will be enrolled to mentor and train less experienced artists. Xross-Polynation has a history of 25 years, which will be the foundation of the message we wish to promote. We are planning events based around various forms of art, including martial arts, and visual arts, in India, London, and Manchester.

African art consists of historical and modern paintings, sculptures, textile art, pottery and other visual forms of art created by native or indigenous Africans or originating from the continent of Africa. African art may also include the art of African people living outside Africa, such as African American art, Caribbean art or art that is inspired by African traditions, such as that found in South America. Interestingly, unifying artistic themes are present despite the diversity of African art. These include a focus on the human figure, visual abstraction, and expressive individualism.

My favourite artist is Frank Bowling. He is a painter and art teacher, whose career spans eight decades from the 1950s to the 2020s. He is known for his abstract paintings created on a monumental scale and for his sensory use of colour.

Born in Guyana (then British Guiana) in 1934, Bowling moved to London when he was 19 years old. He studied painting at the Royal College of Art, where he met David Hockney and R.B. Kitaj. After graduating with a silver medal in 1962, he became well-known in the London art scene for his paintings that contained abstract, symbolic, and figurative elements.

Frank Bowling was friends with the Abstract Expressionists. They thought that paint, colours, and patterns were just as important as the people and other things we can recognise in paintings. They aimed to create abstract art that also had expressive or emotional effects. The surrealist idea that art should originate in the unconscious mind inspired them, as did Joan Miró's automatism.

In 1966, Frank Bowling moved to New York, where his 'Map Paintings' of 1967 to 1971 marked his transition to pure abstraction. He began to concentrate on colour and composition, and, instead of the earth pigments he had used in his early paintings, he experimented with bright colours in his preferred medium of acrylic. His style combines abstraction with personal memories.

After returning to London in 1975, Bowling continued to spend time in New York. In the 1980s, his sculptural paintings combined thickly textured canvases with embedded objects, evoking images of geological strata, riverbeds and landscapes. He experimented with pearlescent and metallic paint, gel, and ammonia to create incandescence in his paintings. Notable work from this period included the 'Great Thames' paintings.

Bowling spent the summer of 1984 as a resident artist and teacher at the Skowhegan School of Art in the US state of Maine. He was joined that summer by his close friend Rachel Scott. They went on to live together from 1989, and they married in 2013.

In his most recent artworks, Bowling has combined several different techniques, including stencilling, collage, poured paint, staining, and stitching canvases. **Frank Bowling was the first black artist to be elected a member of the Royal Academy of Arts on May 26th 2005. He received an OBE in 2008 and was knighted in 2020. Frank celebrated his 87th birthday in 2021 and still paints every day in his studio in London.**

What I like about Frank's work is the uniqueness of his pictures and his amazing talent. Not only that, he is also a distinguished gentleman with a humble spirit.

I honestly believe art speaks for itself. Art is beautiful. Art speaks from the heart. Art comes from within. When you look at the human race, you see so many artists playing out their roles in their lives and in society. I have never been an artist myself, but I have seen the work of artists from all over the world and have been very impressed. What I have realised is that each painting is truly unique.

So be creative and real. I believe that art is extremely therapeutic, and I know a lot of people use art as a kind of therapy, especially if they are suffering from a mental health condition or depression. Art brings out the creative side of your life and heals any part of you that is suffering. We have to remember that suffering is part of each of our lives and plays a role in our lives, but let's have the courage to see suffering for what it is.

Is suffering our enlightened state of life? You can see how the human race has been entwined in suffering for many centuries, whether it be war, slavery, genocide, torture or human rights abuses. Art is a real expression to keep our minds calm and at ease. Please try it. What if you could design an art exhibition describing how slavery has impacted the human race? We could have so many talented artists drawing pictures of incredible people in society over the centuries, people who have had an impact on creating a peaceful world for us all to live in. Give artists the space to express how they are feeling on the inside, and, believe me, they will surprise you.

As a public speaker, it would be my duty to explain about this art exhibition, introducing each of the amazing artists and giving information on where they live and what inspired them to become artists. I would have to find out about the amazing lives of all our artists from all over the world. It would be like a celebration of black history and a museum of slavery at the same time. I would love to see the artists' creativity which is so rich. When portraying black history, our aim is to show victory. We celebrate our history that embraces the whole of humanity, to show that we are all united as human beings.

CHAPTER 11

Public Speaking and Mentoring Young People

"Every kid is one caring adult away from being a success story." Josh Shipp

Time to reminisce. In the year 1990, a good friend of mine got married. Who was the best man? Me! And you know what the best man has to do. Give speeches, of course! Well, I prepared as much as I could and have a guess what happened? I stumbled and froze straight on the spot. Everyone said I did well, but deep down I knew I could have done a lot better. That day, I decided I would never give a speech like that again. Certain events and people play an important role in your life at certain stages. For me, that was a turning point in my life.

In 2011, I joined Utility Warehouse. Even though I struggled with the business side, I became a customer of this company because the home products were very cheap, and the customer service was exceptional. I also used to attend the excellent training sessions organised by this company, and I listened to a lot of speakers at these events. All these speakers had achieved high standards of leadership within that company. One day, it hit me like lightning.

While they were talking on stage about their success stories, I said to myself, *Wow I can do that!* Then I realised, *Wow, I would love to do that. I would love to share stories about my life and the challenges I have overcome. I would love to talk about the story of how I have changed myself into the person I have become. I have so much I want to say to inspire people and I want to share it with the world!* Yes, that is what I wanted to do in the future. I wanted to inspire people through my speeches.

Andy Harrington, who is well-known as the 'Jet Set Public Speaker', addresses audiences all over the world. I found out about his live events called 'Power to Achieve' and attended many of his events, gaining a lot of business contacts at them, including my friend Ravinder Kalsi, the CEO of Xross-Polynation. We had so much in common we decided to start working together as business partners through joint ventures (JVs).

I attended a 4-day course at Andy Harrington's Professional Speakers Academy, where I received a Certification in Public Speaking. What did I learn on this course? This course helped me to become very comfortable as a public speaker. As I motivate people, especially young people, I am asking what problem can I solve for my audience.

How do I build trust with a younger audience? The audience have come to hear me speak because they know and trust that I can make a difference in their lives. They know that I have the solution to a problem in their lives.

The main goal when relating to an audience is to establish rapport with them. Rapport is a feeling of mutual warmth and respect. It is a sense that we are on the same crest of a wave, and that I know the audience and they trust in what I say and what I do. In order to establish rapport, I involve the audience in my speech by asking them questions. This allows me to find a common bond with them - something we can all talk about and relate to. It is important to put the audience's needs first if you, as a speaker, are to build trust with them. Therefore, the focus is on the audience rather than me.

When I speak to audiences of young people, I always tell true stories that help me form a bond with my audience. I am transparent and open about my life and my experiences. People in the audience may relate to my stories and think, *Oh, yes, I've experienced that too.* Stories are memorable and always add flavour to a speech. I don't play safe – I bring emotions into my stories, emotions that will touch the audience. When I am speaking, I allow myself to be vulnerable because you never know what doors your stories will open.

Be willing to stand for something or you will fall for anything. Allow people to feel your conviction. Engage with your audience at all times. I have a social media site and a website about young people, truth, and justice. I will share my website link at the end of this book and my contact information so that readers can get in touch.

Over the past decade, I have had the experience of mentoring and coaching so many people, and to be honest, there is no point in asking someone if they are a good mentor or coach. It is better to ask the mentee if their mentor has helped them change their life for the better.

To me, one of the most rewarding aspects of mentoring young people is bringing out the best in them. During the mentoring process, they discover strengths that they never knew they had. They become more empowered to make decisions. They have more motivation to take action that will improve their lives. Above all, their self-belief and self-confidence increase as they realise that they can achieve their goals and move forward in life.

At the beginning of the mentoring process, I find that asking questions is a good way of getting to know a young person better. However, it's extremely important to truly listen to their answers and to hear exactly what they are saying. This may be different from what you think they are saying! If I'm not sure if I've understood, I ask extra questions to clarify my understanding. I may also pick up on non-verbal cues and empathise with the situation the young person finds themselves in. It may take some time before the young person trusts me enough to open up and tell me about some of the problems or challenges they are facing. One good way of building trust is to share stories of my own life experiences. Often, young people can relate to these and may wish to share similar experiences with me.

We can all learn from the experiences of others. I make it clear that I'm not here to judge but to support and guide the young person in the choices they make. If they are struggling to cope with personal or academic issues, we discuss these and develop some strategies for dealing with them. If the young person needs some practical advice, I will offer ideas based on my own experience and knowledge. If, on the other hand, they just need encouragement, support, and someone to talk to, I will be that person who listens to their concerns, that person who cares about their future, that person who encourages them to develop their skills so that they can grow into the best version of themselves.

I may guide a young person to develop the skills they will need in both their personal and work lives. For example, communication skills are essential in both these areas, whatever field of work they choose. They may also need help with developing negotiation skills to increase their confidence when dealing with a range of people in their personal lives and at work. Another area in which I often help is with practising job interview skills. We role-play an interview. I ask some potential interview questions, while the young person answers. I give my feedback on those answers, and this helps the young person to boost their confidence and increase their chances of being offered the job following a successful interview.

If a young person needs help with finding suitable work or embarking on a particular career, we discuss the best way forward, and I help them set goals and an action plan. After they start working towards these goals, I am there to offer emotional support and motivation when they encounter setbacks. I can also help with job applications or advise them on how to take the next step forward. I may also introduce them to someone I know if I think that person would be a useful contact for my young mentee.

What makes a professional mentoring relationship work is if both the mentor and mentee have learned from each other in the relationship. Have they both grown together? Because that is a successful relationship built on bonding and trust.

CHAPTER 12

No Pain, No Gain

"Life's most persistent and urgent question is, 'What are you doing for others?'" Martin Luther King Jr.

So, now we have touched on it, why it is important to be a Professional Expert Authority? Well, it shows you can be trusted in society and work alongside anyone within any given circumstance. After you have read this book, will you see me as a Professional Expert Authority? Only you can decide that.

I feel I have experienced a lot of hardships, especially growing up in Manchester. The pain of being bullied at school and experiencing racism at such a young age. The pain of my education and how it affected me in society. The pain of my drug addiction and how I overcame this. I have had the courage to share these experiences with you, just to let you know that you can achieve anything if you put your mind to it. But does this qualify me to be a Professional Expert Authority in society? Only you can decide that.

So, let us look at the word 'professional' first. What does it mean? A professional is someone who displays high levels of expertise and efficiency, according to Peter Johnson, HR partner at Cassons, an accountancy company. If you work and behave competently, respectfully, and reliably, other people will regard you as a professional.

The term professional refers to anyone who earns their living from performing an activity that requires a certain level of education, skill, or training. Types of professionals include accountants, teachers, technicians, labourers, commercial bankers, engineers, and lawyers.

Professional people have extensive knowledge of their profession or area of expertise. Please notice I didn't say, 'They know everything.' They stand for something. This is about ethics and having a moral compass.

Professional people keep their word. This is a big one! They are honest. I know this should go without saying, but we all know that there are people who struggle with honesty. Last but by no means least, professional people support others.

The Merriam-Webster dictionary defines professionalism as: "The skill, good judgement, and polite behaviour that is expected from a person who is trained to do a job well." According to Universities UK et al., "Professionalism is commonly understood as an individual's adherence to a set of standards, code of conduct or collection of qualities that characterize accepted practice within a particular area of activity."

All professions adhere to the same universal ethical principles, according to MVOrganizing. These include obeying the law, accountability, respecting others, being honest, loyal and trustworthy, and doing good whilst avoiding hurting others.

According to Quizlet, the six traits of professionalism are: be the best, be dependable, be a team player, be respectful, be ethical, and be positive.

So, let's look at the word 'expert' now. What does 'expert' mean? The Merriam-Webster dictionary's definition is: "having, involving, or displaying special skills or knowledge derived from training or experience." If you're looking for a word to describe an expert, you could use adept to describe their skill level. Alternatively, they could be described as skilled, accomplished, talented, proficient, skilful or gifted.

The Lifespan Development course from Lumen Learning states: "Expert thought is often characterized as intuitive, automatic, strategic, and flexible."

How does an expert differ from a professional? According to Chris Lawrence, a security consultant with TPS, "An expert demonstrates specialized knowledge in thefield in which one is practicing, while a professional displays a high standard of ethics, behaviour, and work activities while carrying out one's profession."

I believe that anyone can become an expert in anything if they dedicate themselves to learning. First, you need to find out what subjects you are interested in. There is no point in becoming an expert in an area that bores you. Next, concentrate on one subject at a time. Learn by studying, practising what you are learning, and teaching or presenting your knowledge to others. However, becoming an expert takes a lot of time. It may take thousands of hours of study, practice, and teaching.

Now we come to the word 'authority'. What Is an authority? The Merriam-Webster dictionary defines 'authority' as the power to influence or command thought, opinion, or behaviour. It also defines authority as "the confident quality of someone who knows a lot about something or who is respected or obeyed by other people."

An authority can also be a person, people or organisation in command, specifically, the government or a local authority. Authority is also defined as a person who is considered an expert in his field. A philosophy scholar who publishes books is an example of an authority.

The website Marketing91 states that there are 13 different types of authority, including expert authority, academic authority, charismatic authority, founder authority, legal governing authority, organisational position authority, ownership authority and prophetic authority.

What are the characteristics of authority? Legitimacy, dominance, informality, rationality, and accountability are the characteristics of authority, according to the website, Sociology Discussion.

So there you have it, I have shared with you what a Professional Expert Authority's traits are, only you can decide the outcome. The gain for me is that I have learned and adapted to so many different job opportunities and business ventures. I have been successful in everything that I have done.

What you have to remember about being an authority is that it's not about you being perfect in business. Instead, it's about having the ability to bounce back from the knocks and setbacks you will undoubtedly experience. It's about learning from your past mistakes. It's about making mistakes very quickly so you can rectify those mistakes and make new decisions that will move you forward.

2017 was a challenging year for me. I had three setbacks, but I knew I was going to win in the end, I just had to learn from these setbacks. When you do this, you will see a blossoming in your character.

CHAPTER 13

Equilibrium

"May I stress the need for courageous, intelligent, and dedicated leadership. Leaders of sound integrity. Leaders not in love with publicity, but in love with justice. Leaders not in love with money, but in love with humanity. Leaders who can subject their particular egos to the greatness of the cause." Martin Luther King Jr.

So, are you now prepared to go on your journey through life? The question I would like to ask is, 'How do you see your life?' As an exhilarating adventure? Or dull and monotonous? I know which option appeals to me. Life is never perfect, and I know it's full of incidents that sometimes we do not want to face up to. I honestly believe in the phrase, God loves a trier, depending on your faith, or you could be from another religion or philosophy of life. In my practice of chanting, we say take action, which leads to painstaking efforts. These efforts produce results that help you grow and move your life in a positive direction.

Do something. Even if it is only the smallest or minutest step, take that action, and great results will come from your efforts. Do we have the courage to learn from our mistakes? Do we have the courage to pick ourselves up when we get knocked down? That's where the magic lies.

So, let's look at my favourite word, *equilibrium*. What does this word mean to you?

Dictionary.com defines equilibrium as: "A state of rest or balance due to the equal action of opposing forces; equal balance between any powers, influences, etc.; equality of effect; mental or emotional balance: equanimity." An example of the latter meaning is: "The pressures of the situation caused her to lose her equilibrium."

I want to give you an example of why we all need equilibrium in our lives, and I honestly believe some of the most successful entrepreneurs have mastered the art of equilibrium.

So why is equilibrium important to me as a **Professional Expert Authority?** Let's look at all the skills I am learning to master:

- Social media expert - Facebook, Instagram, YouTube and Daily Motion.
- Mentor – I have achieved ILML8 Accreditation covering business, leadership, lifestyle, spiritual and self/personal development, and relationships.
- Coach – I have achieved ICA Accreditation.
- Public speaking – I have achieved a Certification in Public Speaking from Andy Harrington's Professional Speakers Academy.

- Toastmasters (public speakers' organisation) - two awards for best speech.
- Teacher and educator - Arts and Culture, History.
- Teacher and educator of 15- to 25-year-olds through workshops, webinars, seminars, events and online courses.
- Consulting Agency - healthy foods, fitness and public relations.

As you can see, I have a lot to do in many different areas of my life. Therefore, I need to divide my time in such a way that working and studying are balanced with calmness. Every day, I make time for chanting. That gives me the physical, mental, and intellectual strength and stamina to do everything else I need to do. I would not be able to achieve my goals if I did not lead a balanced life.

Other virtues of equilibrium are being gentle, calm and steady. This isn't easy, so effort, practice and dedication are essential if you want to master this world. Tenacity is also needed to break through the obstacles, hiccups and hurdles you will encounter as you move through life.

We all need help and support, but what if you found the right person to help you to succeed in your skills and profession? A guide, someone to pick you up when you are down, someone to kick you up the backside when you are procrastinating. Listen to me - we are all guilty of this, and that's why I am highlighting this evermore. Always ask for help and never give up because - remember this - you will be inspiring so many more people than you could ever imagine - this is a mark of a genius.

My passion for working with 15- to 25-year-olds reminds me of the lessons I had to learn in life while growing up and the difficulties and choices I faced. Young men sometimes make the wrong choices just out of peer pressure or the desire to fit into groups or society. The lessons they learn through these choices can be painful but can also show them if they have the steely character to make it through the concrete jungle. My life experience is actual proof for young people, to show them I am not here to patronise, but to demonstrate to them that anything is possible with a little help and the right people around at the right time. Timing is crucial and it certainly was for me. Everyone knows the importance of time because we can never get time back. The clock is always ticking, and it certainly was for me. If we don't reach young people in time, it may be too late.

What if I could use all my life experiences to tell young people not to make the same mistakes as I did? To give them a shortcut to avoid difficult situations and difficult people. Then again, they do say dealing with difficult people is a mark of a true leader. All my life I have had to deal with difficult people, so I can give hope to people who feel hopeless in their lives. The older I get, the more important I feel this is. The more responsible I feel for my own life, the more responsible I feel for other people's lives.

In October 2009, my local SGI-UK community began to hold 'Victory over Violence' meetings. This youth-led campaign was set up in the USA in 1999, and its aim is to tackle the alarming increase in youth-related violence through dialogue, understanding and action. I attended the 'Victory over Violence' meetings on the first Wednesday of every month, knowing that people all over the world were meeting on the same day with the same aim – to create a culture of peace. It was wonderful to be part of a worldwide organisation that was working together to deal with the issue of violence in youth culture.

The meetings made me realise that the gang violence, drugs culture, racism and bullying I had grown up with were continuing in my community. They strengthened my desire and my resolve to help build a better and safer environment for our children to grow up in.

In 2012, I met a gentleman by the name of James Gregory, who also wanted to reduce violence and make Manchester a better place to live. James was introduced to me by a friend, we connected instantly, and our friendship grew from there. At that time, James was setting up his charity, Fathers Against Violence. I was very influenced by the name of the charity, and I decided to go to the open day in the Moss Side area of Manchester. This was one of the best decisions I have ever made, and I realised very quickly why this charity had been set up. James' son had been killed in Manchester in 2009 when he was just 16, so I could understand the pain James was going through. James knew he had a mission to carry out in his son's name, which is the right action to take with love and compassion.

The main aim of Fathers Against Violence is to provide teenage boys and young men with more male role models, who they can turn to for encouragement, support and guidance. This should prevent young people from becoming involved in violence and crime.

Fathers Against Violence helped me change my life. I realised there are people in the world who want to stand up for justice and make the world a better place. The charity runs various activities, enabling young people to become involved in something positive and giving them the strength to say no to joining a gang or taking drugs. It aims to encourage young people in different areas of Manchester to pursue a better world away from drugs or gang violence, which is so common in the city. It helps young people to realise that they have strengths, which they can develop, and that there are opportunities for everyone, even those whose don't have much money. One of the projects James set up is called *'Can U Kick It?'* It is a football project helping youths and underprivileged kids to seek a better life through football and sport.

I knew immediately that I wanted to support James and become involved in the excellent work that Fathers Against Violence was doing. As we developed the charity, we faced several setbacks. People could be openly hostile, coming into our office, criticising us and accusing us of not doing enough to help young people.

During that time, I continued to chant and practice SGI-Buddhism. While studying a Buddhist text, I read a quotation from Nichiren Daishonin, the Buddhist priest and philosopher on whose teachings Soka Gakkai International (SGI) is based. It made me realise that the setbacks were arising as a direct result of all the effort I was making to transform my own life and that of my local community. Seeing the setbacks for what they were – negative influences that were attempting to prevent me from moving forward – I continued to chant daily, and this allowed me to transform my anger and frustration into courage and compassion. My belief that I was on the right path continued to grow, despite the challenges James and I faced. We were both growing as people in the midst of these setbacks. Carrying on with perseverance and persistence, we gradually began to see positive results. As an increasing number of men volunteered to become mentors, we were able to help more young people avoid a life of violence and crime.

When you meet certain people and you have the same passion and beliefs, it's strange how events in your life can take a turn for the worse. My daughter, Candice, had a stepbrother who was murdered in 2014. At this difficult time, my faith became deeper as I dedicated myself to the practice of chanting. I was determined to bring value out of this tragic incident.

I was determined to transform poison into medicine, so I chanted a lot, read Buddhist scripture, and was supported by all the members of my local SGI-UK community, who chanted for me and encouraged me to believe that the murderer would be brought to justice.

I am more determined than ever to create a world where everyone can live in peace. The death of our son and brother has encouraged me to do more to help young people and make a difference in the community. I have been inspiring all men, whether they are fathers or not, to act as role models for the younger generation.

As you can see, I have some very special people in my life who have helped me become the leader I am today. It is a matter of taking one step at a time to fulfil your dreams and that is the process I am following. The people I have mentioned in this book are playing a major role in my life to develop my entrepreneurial skills, so that I can become a thought leader who can make a difference in the world. Now I hope you can understand the word *equilibrium* and why it is so important to live with harmony and composure in your life. I would like to dedicate this book to all the people in my life who are helping me become successful in my chosen field. You are all an inspiration to me, and I hope to serve you all well.

As a life coach and mentor, my passion is transforming the lives of young people so that they can be the leaders of the 21st Century. I do this by delivering exceptional workshops, seminars and webinars. As a professional mentor and coach, I use my skills and life experience to help young people even more, so they know I am a trusted authority in society.

Now I am a lot older, I realise we were taught the wrong values when we were younger. Time for self-development and for me to work on myself to be the best version of me that I possibly can be. Time for total transformation, a revolution of my own life and spirit. I honestly believe that faith and spiritual beliefs will play a big role in people's lives in the future years, and I do believe this is what has kept me going and protected me throughout my turbulent life. It's been like being on a rollercoaster.

So, what does the future hold? I have this dream, this determination, this goal, to inspire one million entrepreneurs over the next 40 years in the UK. I will fulfil this dream with a little help from my friends. With the skills and expertise I have, I will create so much value in the world to make it a better place.

I plan to deliver exceptional workshops, seminars, webinars and online courses on leadership skills for young people aged from 10 to 25. I aim to build a global brand that I can take around the world. What about taking public speaking around the world as a jet set speaker? I am sure that would be exciting and exhilarating! Sharing your passion with the world would be an amazing journey in your life, too. Do you dare to dream big?

Sometimes, it's better to start small with baby steps first, especially if you have a mission statement to create something tangible in the world. Helping to create a better world for everyone to live in gives your life a deeper meaning. Are you living out your mission statement? Are you following your calling by opening up doors to create your success? They say that if your dreams do not scare you, they are not big enough.

So, how big are your dreams?

As a public speaker, it's important that your audience already knows you as a person through your books. I think this can take a lot of pressure off you because the audience knows and trusts you from the beginning. This is especially important when working with children and teenagers. They need to see their mentor as a trusted person in society.

Writing children's books on leadership is a niche I would love to explore in future. These would be for an audience of children and teenagers aged between 10 and 15, accompanied by parents. This is an impressionable age when many young people turn to drinking alcohol, taking drugs or committing violence, often because of peer pressure and a lack of positive role models. I would like to solve their lack of self-confidence with the '3 S's': Self-confidence, Self-development, and Self-esteem.

My Unique Branded Solution (UBS) is a formula to help young people transform their lives. It is called the Dynamic Dream Formula:

D = Development – self/personal development

R = Relationships

E = Education

A = Association

M = Motivation

This is the formula I have used to transform my life. I live by it, and it has served me well throughout my life. I want to share it with as many young people as possible.

I also plan to set up an online magazine called *Global Men*, which will unite successful, professional men around the world. This magazine is designed to help men raise their awareness of who they are as people and to think about why they do what they do. It will help men to explore their roles, whether it is as an entrepreneur, intrapreneur, infopreneur, innerpreneur, CEO, director or manager. It will explore such topics as money, asking how you can create value in society with your money. Small business development will also be covered, exploring how you can create a big future for your small business. *Global Men* also plans to run mastermind classes to help men succeed in their chosen field and produce short films on successful men to inspire others.

Moving forward, I will use equilibrium in my life to create value and to live a balanced life for everyone's benefit. This is actual proof that equilibrium can help people succeed at the top of their field of expertise. I imagine myself speaking on stage to around 10,000 young people, inspiring them to reach their goals which I know they are capable of achieving. My famous quote is:

"STAND FOR SOMETHING OR YOU WILL FALL FOR ANYTHING."

It would be so great to inspire people on stage, a lot of people, showing them how important it is to be true to themselves in all situations. Follow your mission in life and you can't go wrong!

I hope you found this book inspiring and it gives you the insight and all the details on how I have transformed my life and transformed myself into the person I am today. I do believe that, if I can achieve this, so can you, with a little help and guidance along the way. I appreciate you all and hope this book will inspire you to listen to your calling and realise the greatness within you.

ACKNOWLEDGEMENTS

I would like to thank all my family for always being there for me and believing in me.

Heartfelt thanks to a special lady in my life, Margarett Hart, who keeps me focused.

Very special thanks to my mum, Venese Rose Kington. I couldn't have asked for a better mum. She has been a real rock and a tower of strength in my life.

A big thank you to my dad, Franklin Kington, who is a real warrior of a man. He has always been an inspiration to me.

I'd like to thank my elder sister, Jackie, for being a role model in my life, and my younger sister, Jessica, for always being warm and supportive.

Thank you to my brother, Michael, for always being a brother to me. He has turned out to be a fine gentleman – I am proud of him.

To my nephews – you are loved very much.

Thank you to Eddie and Sharon Lewis, my cousins, who have grown up to be responsible adults, and my youngest cousin, Kizzy Roddey, who has turned out to be a fine gentlelady.

A huge, heartfelt thank you to my special friend, James Gregory, who has helped me to write this book.

A big thank you to my business coach, Maria Kompanowski, who has helped me to move to the next level in my entrepreneurial journey and has been a very dear friend to me.

Many thanks to Ravinder Kalsi, who is a gentle lady and a scholar and has always stood by me and believed in me. Your support and encouragement are very much appreciated.

Thank you to all my inspiring business colleagues, who have played an important role in my life, especially Lisa-Marie Igbinovia, who designed the cover of this book.

A big shout-out to my editor and publisher of this book, Roz Andrews of RA Writers For Hire Ltd.

A huge thank you to my special friends Edwina Clare Molloy and Roger Bertrand for always helping and encouraging me on the journey towards writing this book.

There are so many other people I'd like to thank. You've all played an important part in my life. You know who you are.

ABOUT THE AUTHOR

Frankie Kington

Frankie Kington is an entrepreneur, mentor and public speaker. He is passionate about helping and inspiring young people to fulfil their true potential.

After experiencing racism and bullying as a child, Frankie experimented with smoking cannabis, injecting amphetamines known as speed, and taking other drugs during his turbulent teenage years. As a young adult, he felt a sense of hopelessness which led him to smoke crack cocaine.

Despite all the challenges he faced, Frankie turned his life around and found value and a true purpose. His love of learning led him on a variety of paths before he decided to pursue his passion for mentoring and inspiring young people.

Through his seminars, workshops and courses, Frankie nurtures young people's skills and encourages them to overcome the obstacles they inevitably encounter. He empowers young people to make the most of the opportunities open to them and to realise that achieving goals and dreams is possible for everyone, no matter what background they come from or how much money they have. He shares his own powerful story openly in the belief that it will prevent young people from getting caught up in drug abuse, alcohol addiction or violence and crime.

Frankie's mission is to inspire one million young people in the UK over the next 30 years to become the next generation of entrepreneurs and thought leaders. Although he may not be around to see this goal come to fruition, he is determined to get the ball rolling by inspiring 15-to-25-year-olds through his mentoring and coaching programmes.

Find out more about Frankie Kington on his website. Be inspired by the videos on his YouTube channel: Frankie Kington Life Coach Empowering Youth Development and connect with Frankie on LinkedIn. If you would like to get in touch with him, he'd love to hear from you. His email address is:

frankie.lisafruitfulleaders@gmail.com

Printed in Great Britain
by Amazon

78350454R00051